Desdemona's Fire

Desdemona's Fire

Poems by
Ruth Ellen Kocher

Detroit
Lotus Press

International Standard Book Number 0-916418-83-9

Grateful acknowledgment is made to the following publications in
which these poems first appeared: "Poem to a Jazz Man" in *Poet Lore;*
"The Siren's Sound" in *Sojourner;* and *"Mélange:* A Commencement"
in *Ploughshares.*

LOTUS PRESS, Inc.
"Flower of a New Nile"

Post Office Box 21607
Detroit, Michigan 48221

for all of the children halved into existence,
for my mother, who took a chance on me,
my father, who claimed me,
and Coby, who let me be whole

Contents

I

. . . beauty is nothing but the beginning of terror,
which we still are just able to endure.

— Rainer Maria Rilke

Poem to a Jazz Man

My mother doesn't seem to remember
any of this, but the music must have been sweet,
cool jazz taking her like snake charm,
pleasure and desire, a warm July night.
The tall black man at the piano must have teased
the keys into filling that hot air with speak-easy
sugared sounds. She didn't have a chance.
Some poor white girl from the edge of town,
singing Saturdays to pay her rent,
could never have known what the music could do,
how the man and the piano, his fingers, his soul,
could so easily enter her, grow there
into a small, dark-eyed song.

Child, she would say, you are just like him.

Liturgy of the Light-Skinned

On me you can smell a story,
iron and blue slag,
wooden floor boards
danced on all night.
There's a piano in this story
and a black man
whose fingers were not very long.
In the piano are the souls of lizards
who frantically
jump against the keys
seeing a light
they believe is the sun.
The man at the piano
is someone's father but
his daughter is a myth to him.
She is not part of the story.
The ending is not ending
when a woman
meets a child who is
not her own image.
The woman combs her own hair.
The mirror frames her face.
She thinks about the old woman
downstairs, the child at her feet, and wishes
that the lights in the house
would not go out
because the swollen limbs of her mother
have failed again,
but they do, every night
and so every night
the old woman and the young woman

are both mothers, share
the bitter blanket of arthritis
and aching. Darkness.
This is only the beginning.
I am the child and my mother
fights the rage of her mother,
the brimstone scowls at the wicked,
the hard light that passes through
her house. I am the daughter,
the lizard, the man who knows only myth
but thinks he's the sun. My mother looks at me
and I know I am not part of this story.

Mélange: A Commencement

I came to this world on the back
of a white elephant
who carried a talking monkey
on the sloped smoothness of her tusk.
The monkey
would riddle the trees with questions,
ask them
how many pears they shed in the time
it took Monkey to somersault from one
end of the cosmos to the other
and back again, and the trees would respond,
But we shed only plums.
The elephant would plod along
wishing to be somewhere else
and hoping that someday
the gods would take
a considerable weight from her limbs.
I sat on her back like an empty bowl
not knowing the difference from
the Where We Go and the Where We Came.
The birds watched us from the tops
of puzzled trees, screeching *mulatta,*
mulatta, thinking, perhaps, that I was a mule
who should carry the monkey and the elephant instead.
When we reached the river of Where We Are,
the monkey and the elephant
turned into small bitter nuts
that I chewed and mixed
into a marrow I swallowed, a pasty
obligation. As I dove into the river,
I heard behind me the blue macaws calling,
mulatta, mulatta, as if before me
they knew my name.

Sisters

We barely speak
but deep sleep brings you to me
sometimes, sister, your bare wrists
hovering to cover some fright
in your face, so pale,
so white it yearns for grief.

I would bear
the scar on your cheek,
the slash-rip
from glass that marks
your third summer, the drive
on the Jersey Turnpike:
some huge rig wielding
tons of speed at us.
I knew enough to cover, pull
the quilt that wrapped us,
all of my six years lying there,
knowing a danger we didn't know.
You, I'll always see, leaning into it,
glass spraying your face, mouth open
but somehow silent like a feigned horror.

I couldn't protect you, not because
you were my rival in the green years
of our sisters' war, but because
that truck hurled a first truth at us,
a glut of helplessness deep as a bog.
You, I could cocoon,
simple as that, the barreling truck

with you, even as you lay
your own sons down.
Their small heads
in the dark. We are there.

Susquehanna: The Projects

This was a home.
A home of rows separating there and here.
Rows of rooms for three or six of ten.
Rooms of few windows the women looked out.
Windows that faced a four foot yard.
A yard that sprung from culm dust and layers of soot.
Culm and birch streaked white. Streaked black.
Birch woods from waste piles of boxcar dirt.
Waste from coal belts, like giraffes without heads.
Coal belts from factories with their eyes knocked out.
Factories with sulfur stacks claiming the sky.
A sky above maples raging from rust.
Maples grown in ore confessed from the earth.
Ore that cooled near a furnace in weeds.
A furnace of stones carried by hand,
ringed in slag that's evening blue.
Slag that surfaces in heavy rain,
a secret returned from an azure grave.
Rain that fed our river into a bitch that flowed.
A river that swallowed nine hundred homes.
Nine hundred families that needed to sleep.
A sleep that was built into corners and walls.
Corners that made up small, white rooms.
Rows of rooms, and rooms and rooms.
This was a home.

Susan's Hair

There were women who combed
my hair. Brenda Brown. Aunt Charlene Ryan.
Evlyne DeGrafenreid who said Dee-GRAF-en-reeed
like a sweet thing dying on her tongue.

Strong,
black-willed-single-mother-raising-children
kinds of women that sat me down,
raked the first hot combs
through green streaks of Afro-sheen and pomade,
twisted my scalp into corn-rows racing to one
knot at my neck,

all with hair
kept like a duty that would keep them whole
and tightly woven
as the pony-tail plaits,
the tucked bun, the thick, spun
twists of hair.

Susan's grows like mine
though she is as white as the polished egg of a hen.
I search her chin,
her nose, scan the eyes that beam back the blue
flight of a heron scared into frenzied
flapping, search past the long coil of her grandmothers,
the Polish bubbas pale as her
for some dark African
who laid down her course
in Susan's hair.

I know her, the sad New England heart,
the eyes, small mole near the mouth. She is my mother
at 23, lost by her own hands,
                         circular in her movement
as though even the marrow of her bones
should mimic an orbiting path,
                         because she needs to be the resistant,
the untamable but susceptible, like the elements,
like her hair, unable to lie the disposition.

White Boys Who Sing the Blues

When I was twenty
I took home the blonde son
of a potter's wheel,
his golden hand
a charm wound around my breasts,
his tongue
pinkened from a pure summer
of eggplant
and strawberries.
He said
You are a landscape,
as though I had never seen
my own nappy trees,
my own cove
edged into the beach of my sea.
You are a landscape
simple as that, as July
or a fire alarm
ringing us into the streets.
He found me
twisted, the rounded curve
of a question mark streaking
my spine. What did he mean?
Browned like Aztec clay
just scraped from the mountain,
damp muddy bank that hugs a stream—
my breath, the breath of forest,

eyes, a wide ravine
opened
as if by anger, the earth shaking.
His landscape:
brown girl, yellow girl
stumbling from a boulder field,
a canyon-eyed child.

Braiding

I.

Each woman does it differently.
Brinette scolds her children
and weaves the holy ghost into my hair
knowing the difference in my skin
like her own son, large-boned
Creole boy with his daddy's
disposition. She says my name
determined to jog me, *Ruth,*
with emphasis on the fricative motion
of speaking, of women and sisterly
devotion to God and His signs:
that I have come to her
once again, on just the day
she needs cab fare to the AME.
God wants her there.

Long sliver of the right cold inside us,
take us over the fold, the good turn:
how we know everything wants us near,
back again to some comfort
without knowing. World?
Ours, never again.

II.

Kim owns a salon, does "hair design."
Her braiding marks a rhythm in my ear,
her three-inch nails clicking
the tripart criss-cross of Kan-eka-lon strands

while David explains to the next girl
how, the night before in drag,
he does a number at a family club,
loses the rice bags he used for breasts
during a pirouette to Donna Sommers
screeching ". . . hot stuff baby this evening,
hot stuff baby tonight."

This is back street.
Shake that, that mother, damn
all over everything you ever said
and want it back again
back where we belong,
take us there. Take us.

Kim says, Girl, you gotta big head,
and charges me more than she said,
takes a break and eats lunch
while the other girls' men
come in, one by one, for waves.

III.
All October. Orange mornings
and brown leaves and boyfriends calling
girl, calling you away from home
as if the woods would love you better.
Billy Joe. Billy Joe's hands.

My mother sent me to Brenda Brown's,
a neighborhood black lady, because
she'd know what to do with my hair,
would know the depth,
the hold of it. Brenda smoked cigarettes,

sat me down with her own kids
all munching Sugar Pops,
let the comb stew in the flame
so that, when she finally touched it
red hot to slicked down nap,
the heat would evaporate Afro sheen into breath,
hair into smoke that choked me all day.
She called my friend "Lily girl,"
colorless besides freckles that startled her face,
taught her how to do it,
how to move the comb
carefully away from you
like a brand turned over
and over until you're
ready to go.

When you're ready to know
why you always ran
go back again and listen ,
voices, voices, all over you
taking the blanket of shadows,
all of their hands,
twisting the dark fold into a message:
hieroglyphic artifact of your own
wanting. Say it again,
you love me. You love my hair,
all coarseness and telling.

I have walked
into my neighborhood to look for the paper,
look for the casualty that names this day:
brother, sister, friend.
I am not a housewife,
not the hermetic secret of jelly jars and television,
the crippled widow next door
but trace the paths of my home
as if they were the spine of a lover I've dreamed,
a bloody, bruised and limp burden of body without soul:

my home, my prison-house.

Near the flattened
body of a mocking-bird chick
thrown over by an indifferent breeze,
I find the paper and clip out their names,
their brief histories and gray scale photos:
Debbie O'Boyle, Cory Steele, Bobby Hunter,
remembering that we have only
ourselves and a slim promise of wind,
sun and evening,
perhaps, rain.

I am a young black woman who,
on Tuesday morning, hears in the trees
the circular sound of her own heart,
the rhythm of her youth a bludgeoned
repetition, a sound-bite barking
a single thought. Live. Live. Live.

Searching for the Zebra Finch

— for A.S.

Your brother has died.
You can come to this moment as it was,
the way fire smacked back against the snow
so that the whole yard of the trailer
seemed saved, finally, by orange light.
You can come slowly, backwards, knowing
the synchronicity of your small offering
melting through thin ice while a man goes
suddenly into sleep, remembering you, again.
You can go back to the cage door,
open and swinging, scattered feathers
and the nest, broken, the cat, missing.
The evening, another and another loss.
When you doubt what you know
search endlessly, as if you never found him
wedged behind the sofa, folded into his own wings
and the shattered form a lie takes when the story
has ended. Somewhere within this zero degree memory
you hold a small boy to your chin and pretend he is
your own son, that his face is your face and he lives
because you say his name. You may even go
a different direction, to another city
where orange blossoms sicken you
to a point of forgetting only to turn a corner
and find yourself, standing in the snow,
watching the funeral pyre of a cage bird
as though a ceremony could keep you
from the flutter of zebra finches mating.
Hate the moon if you need to. She has never

loved you. Give up on not smoking.
When your hands are empty, they close into fists.
Curse the crocuses before they ever breathe.
The world is littered with too many flowers.
But come back to this moment, to a small flight
twisted into the palm of your hand,
into the grieving crevice of your hand.
Let it pierce you like a thorn. Remember:
an open door and a cold evening,
the fire and the snow. Come to yourself,
to the silence, and to the cat, sleeping.

The Last

I am ironing my black vest
noticing how the silk has frayed,
how the beaded embroidery
undoes itself
as if even my clothes have become tired
of mourning.

I have written too many elegies,
cast, too far into the wind,
these names of leaving—
not even my own
but a grip still bound by aching.

I have written too many
and said their names like syllables,
regret the charge of my tongue,
the motion of mouth to memory.
Too many

elegies for morning
and a sand scraped child, and a boy
who said my name
like *sister*
and a girl with red flame for hair
and again, again.

Palace Cleopatra

One morning you wake
to discover you have become a god,
the goddess of forever
whose hair crowns a thousand daughters
etched into the surface
of their fathers' tombs.
Your arms yellow into jaundice
when the sun sets,
creeps away in the far reaches
of wintering, your brother
gone home. Your lover,
your doom.
Years from now
in twenty feet of water
a man discovers
this sovereign of the obscure,
speaks your name
as if in death you are
more desirable,
wonders
if before you went back, once again
to the riddled lash of serpent's tongue,
you thought of Adam
and the animals
wondering their names.
A man studies you,
determines that thirty men
painted your portrait,
filled the rooms
of the palace with your eyes,
just off, so that their gaze

of your gaze would be ours also,
these centuries gone.
You are the archeologist's
thin nightmare,
that last bite, the final utterance
whose self
herself knew. Your name
his doom. His everyday
finding you—
in sleep, in the sugar
lurking in the cupboards,
wandering through his rooms
mortal, and found.

Desdemona's Fire

Birth, not death, is the hard loss. — Louise Glück

Trace the image
of yourselves,
dark arm, white thigh.
That the two of you
could have a child
is my story.
Imagine her,
child in a red nightgown
sleepwalking through the center
of her mother's kitchen
looking for the dog
she never had:
poor moor, poor she
as me, that other life
that came from you.

I am writing myself into your story,
not as a dream, not as the hierophant
whose silk robes drape over your feet
like white-water tide spilling. I am yours,

the alien hand.

Call me daughter
and you will be saved.
Call me wind that feeds your fire.
Call me water. Call me breath.

I am writing myself into your story
because you murder again
not knowing my birth.

If you spoke
as though you loved me,
strangers would forget
how we pass each other in the littered
morning,
fail among the milk cartons
and crushed cans rusted
into their cores.

Say it simply:
your eyes reflected in mine
as though our other lives
were not this one also.

What alien hand
keeps you splitting yourselves in two,
determined to create a life
that turns one morning toward the sink
and above the pitch of a radio,
sees her own reflection,
the dark circle of her own name:
girl in a red nightgown
who speaks
an ancient alphabet in her sleep.

Say it finally: the alien hand
that destroys your so many ways.

II

*There are questions which
people who have everything
ask people who have nothing
and they do not understand.*

—Bruce Weigl

Yellow Girl

Yellow girl, I see you sitting in a car that idles next to mine
at an intersection like any in this city, wide and indistinct.
Your hair is the musty color of butterscotch. Your eyes,
mine twenty-eight years ago, uncaught by distinctions,
naming. A rock is a rock, a tree, a tree as any other.

A car is meant to take you home. A name is meant to keep
you there.

Who is this man? Workshirt. Do you recognize his red hair,
know blueness as him? Who is this man, the oiled hands,
fingers flat from engines, wrenches, rough from sandpaper
grit and concrete? Know him, this white man, this black man
is yours, this car, this intersection, all yours in an idling
moment when the red turns green and you go forward,
away, into the life you have. A new life. You call it *Father*.

Everywhere, your hair is deep, black and woolly thick.
Twisted. Long plaits woven by your grandmother's hands.
Evenings, you sing songs, chase the moths beneath porch
lights, letting your long red nightgown drag the grass
enough to dampen the hem. Yellow girl, your eyes are
amber fish scales, your skin, red clay but deeper brown.
Your hair, mild as the beige of cork, the beige of autumn,
the sand beige wetness of tide. Beige is your home.

Neighbors sleep but know your name in the blueness of
winter mornings before the school bus comes. Alleyways
circle the life you call evening and morning and noon. You
are safe: television and backyard fences. A sister who is

blonder than you. Pale girl. Daddy's girl. You are mirror,
name, the face I know of who we are: Esu the guide,
daughter of pyramids, all continents hungry for being. You
are Odysseus the traveler saying, "I am here." You are
Christ the carpenter finally waking, saying, "I am."

Are you looking for home again? The long walk up to the
door. The well in front with horseshoes lining the sides, all
pointed upward for good luck. Imagine the road winds just
before the gate, the trees obscure each car until they wind the
hill and disappear. Red cars. Blue cars. Barely a glimpse of
each and then the long green throat of the woods swallows
each one whole. The woman who stands in the doorway
knows you, knows your name and thinks, "Why isn't she
coming?"

Beyond this house is a hill then another and another. Are
you home? There is a fire hydrant in another town. The
water presses tall sprays from the blunt arms, painted to
resemble a man, a cartoon face with a fire hat. Water skids
over the street and lifts oil from the pores of the road, paints
spectrum on your feet. Run through. The water touches your
skin and turns ashy brown into wet olive that traces the
splash on your leg. Yellow girl, your eyes: coal deep
magnets that pull the world into you, vortices of space. Your
mother is warm earth, soft. Your mother is the pale peach of
summer orchard, the pink bud of oleander, round
smoothness of chestnut. You are mothered by goose down
whiteness, fathered by possibilities. Breathe. Breathe
deeply. Yellow girl, child. Go home.

Long days bring the dusk into your room, right to your feet.
Three nights ago, you cringed. Nigger girl, who are you?
The afternoon is hot skin. Swells like the promise of

heartbreak, the call from behind that you ignore—the last breath. You cannot breathe. You never breathe, as though existence choked you from the beginning. Here is your story.

The moment their hands touched you came into being. Mother. Father. You. Your spine curves like a fish, a tadpole—curves like the road to their home. The bridge near the river near the furthest mountains of their lives. You, your father's father, blue tinged deep in the eye, green in your hands and wondering, always, wandering. Wandering. You, his own mother, soft footed and sure of the path. You, your mother's mother, her father too, broken splinters of light that break up morning, black knees of the wilderness finding itself again. Taste this, like the truth that springs from pine sap. Taste the tin electric tinge seizing your tongue, the sharp gusts filling and leaving your lungs. Breathe. Yellow girl, I know you. I know.

My Mother as Daedalus

In the way the poets see Icarus
build the dense stroke in Brueghel,
the red life of brown only in the underneath,
my mother comes through me,
her hands, the wide swing of my hips,
the indifference to lost narratives of fathers
and sons who are too ambitious
even in small matters of flight,
light and doom, a present
absent of past but heavy with it also
like each pink pocket of pregnancy—
how we tore through her
until, half dead and bloodied,
she would kiss us anyway,
save each first shoe.

Or was it Prometheus
who made his mother weep at the rash
dash to fire in a HUD labyrinth of project-homes:
no back doors, no porches, no
windows that would let her out.
A mother crying in a rented
bedroom that was most of her house.

Her, I remember.

No, it *was* Icarus
and he was a she, a girl
not thin or white or innocently
dumb and foolish but searching

like a moth to the lid of a jar,
a punctured light the painter hasn't seen,
nor the poet—not a bird but an urge
the mother remembers into being.
Imagine that, a girl with wings
like her mother's hands
moved by the same tiring want
so the fall becomes the better fate,
a knowing of heat by breasts
curved into the spiral down.
And as women would, they go
together, her mother falling too,
a twin birth and death of desire.

Flowers for Aurelia

This woman is praying.
Because the sea is a blue blinding her
into submission, her weak arms wound
around her own waist, wanting. Because the sky
has again given her over to another day filled
with the spoiled scent of clams rotting in the sun
and the hungry screech of sea birds
flying toward the azimuth,
                flocking to the compulsion
that has steered them since birth.

She jumps from the small boat that has barely
brought her this far from beach
leaving behind
                the thick red breath of begonia,
wind flowers threatening each morning
with severe and lasting fuchsia, the fringe
of violet at the edge of her yard.

                She swims
downward into green ovals of carolina jasmine
and the bubbling of her own life leaving
her lungs. Swims downward past red bundled
pyrocanthus and honeysuckle sloped forward
pointing her deeper
until
                there at the bottom
she finds her own name.

The light draws her
          upward.
The brine of her own birth
presses into her with the sea smell
of her mother, the large hands of her father
seeming now like secret oysters
opening,
          so that she reaches into the green
fold of her own morning, past the silver
darts of minnows, the lapped current of sun
and water, wanting nothing.

          The nothingness
of air. The bad breeze that whips into
the noon time of desert dune.
          Because she cannot recall
having ever been hungry
she breaks water. She flails the boat.
She climbs aboard with her hands empty.

Asthma

Stinking fish
line the beach
as far as I can see,
both ways winding off
in silver steps to an old tire and
a rusty muffler whose stretch of pipe
protrudes: the rough spine
of a prehistoric reptile
just now come up
from the depths
to breathe.
If I wait long enough,
anything may wash up
onto the shore.

The old men who live here
become obsessed,
every day checking beach deposits,
lugging each piece of junk
up the hang of the beach
into backyard piles of sea salvage.
I have their same need
to bring things back to
my porch in summer,
sealed in jars, lids punctured
so I hear the last
spasms of small life
flick glass.

These men take their answers
from the sea as I wait, belly up,

beached like the fish
in their deaths, wait
for the day to have me
stay or go, dress or sleep,
call my name.
Perhaps a new mother,
or lover, will stand up
from the tide, see the bulk of me
here and preach of women
who would not pretend
any small breath
could plant a secret
in the sea, something forgotten
long enough so that we
know we need it
and the knowing
is not enough to drag
it back through
the sand in sacks.

Water

I missed the lesson on uplifting
blackness—the yes ma'm no ma'm
I don't live here but ask me anyway
lesson of patience and growing old,
pepper and salt under a Sunday hat
with canary bows, the function of spirituals
exorcising madness and sadness
so that my face in the sun would be warm
and round, and dark dark brown,
dark dark I mean of the singular things,
the heart, the liver, the spleen:
what keeps you going—

the blessing of my birth,
that I can see through it
makes me wonder what
they've sold me. Clear thoughts.
Cold resolution malted with prayer.

I missed the hour of my soul's
deliverance—the son who knows the father's name.
Us, the dove, rising from the stream—three of us
Brother John touching our knees,
delivered from his own distraction towards life
and the knowing pull of it, wanting life
more than water or white
wings taking home the whole of his want:
lifted, clouds, cirrus, Babel-bound—
saved slaves who knew the wood clutch of a tree
and all its fruit, wanton. One more wanting
as though the water, when poured over their skulls,
lit through—until they found
no sweetness in losing.

The Girl Gymnast

Are you
all of our mistakes,
our hunger,
determination girl?
What about air?
Do you eat only this,
breathe,
sleep?
Are you taken
by this, by the air
last night
the way the wind
is no one's friend
leaving the lake to think
by reflection that she
is actually sky?
Are you hungry or
are you the reflection,
the sky itself, the galactic
belly of spirals
seeming to fill darkness
only from very far away,
from down here
where real space closes
the plane by which
we connect small points
into form:
Hercules,
The Three Sisters,
Cassiopeia
suspended in mid-air.

Are you hunger?
Do you sleep in the space
between your ribs
or do you palpate the turn
even now, even in this dark dream
I give you . . .
Are you lonely
for weight, for shoes
that will weigh you firmly
to the ground where a step
is being?
Can we keep you?
Do you speak,
do you eat, do you breathe or
are you only
for sky,
for the fixed outline
of form,
the small constellations
of your thigh, your cheek,
your hand mapped
into the astronomer's mind
just now, as you evaporate
into your own might.
Girl, can we see you?

Message from the Snowbound Girl

She dreams she
wakes to find Lazarus
wandering through her rosebed
wiping his thorn torn skin
with astonishment at his own bleeding.
Even I am more adorned with grief than he,
holding himself, clutching his own ribs
with the even temperament of a lover
come back to a lover again.
It seems the sun
has me remember her remember him,
her face braced in Northeast winter as though
she were the brittle gray surface of sky,
the laconic February morning
as it drifts in. Can I forget my memory
of myself, forget her singing,
forget the ebbed swell of paired doves
that rose in her throat as if she could die
with the shrill carriage of high C,
the cascade of octaves
bridging her with the passive
infinity of air? Listen.

I cannot stand the snow.
I hate the sound of birds in winter.

My voice is her voice, dead, dry leaves
huddled at the base of dormant trees
bare in their branches. How a hospital room
has changed me, changed a yellow
stretch of being from dogwood bloom

41

and the brightness of deep
spring woods into a single splintered
morning as though the details,
the long orange slug
climbing the black length of tree,
a dead kingfisher and the broken
nest of a rose finch have all been forgotten.
She's left herself again,
left for the delusion of wild phlox
and cattail banks, for the tall
pine as if it had undone
each of its fists and would surrender
sprays of pollen into this day
just for her—
just because she assumes each breath,
each moment. Inwardness.
The relief of exhalation:
a faulting faith the living have.
Listen. I hear her tell me once more,
tell herself grown a decade older, to fall down.

Fall to your knees.

Fall into the shadow of leaving,
the short eruption of this life
as a doorway to somewhere
we've already been, to the dogwood,
a rosebed, to a stretch of thorns
and Lazarus wondering.

Talking with The Buddha

In this house I am not ugly — Lewis Turco

—for N.D.

I've met you as a monk
near a mountain stream
guiding me past shrouded
pilgrims who died in ochre robes,
found you
in a world of rain.
You knew me as if
you knew again
the trees were lost
around us.

      Imagine
the eruption of dogwood
in the palm of your hand
and your breath
sick and heavy like the breath
of blooms.
      I'm dying like this,
with my eyes closed,
in dreams of milk
as skin smooth bareness,
as mad white moments
and so on.

You've come as a boy
come back again
from a dark deep cave
laughing when I call

your name,
as a wave moving
my lungs to fight,
a tortoise carrying me
home alone,
the ghost of a god
who haunts
each room in the small house
I remember.

You, I know
as a moment .
I know as waking.

   Imagine both your hands
crippled
by the spread
of magnolia flowers,
so that you can touch
nothing else.
   I'm living like this,
in the narrow evening,
in mad white moments
where my arms
atrophy
in yellow moss
and lotus leaves,

where my tongue
is seized by dahlia blooms
so that we speak only
in asking *Who
are you?* You live
like this. You wait
for the questions.

The Siren's Sound

Maybe because we've reached
the millennium,
or because my body catches
the draft of memory
that harbors violence
like an Atlantic wave
repeatedly breaking, I woke
last night
to the sound of trumpets sustained
far off in unison,
expecting next
the hoof beats of horses
riding into my room,
four men and four beasts
wiping the ground from beneath me.
I'd forgotten the weeks of my youth
praying
for warning because I have always
only wanted to be saved.
I have always only wanted to be ushered
from the row houses where
my childhood lives, no matter what.
I don't know why
they changed their minds,
replaced the distant apocalyptic call
with the usual hum of the refrigerator,
the whisper of the fan circling above my head
like an open eye, but they turned back,
the night cloaked to their shoulders,
trailing behind them in the wind

so that morning was naked
and tentative. Later, in the elevator
I could hear the wild hearts of strangers
fighting for their lives.

The Watering Stone
—for B.W.

I.

I can tell you this:
every night
for a year
I dreamt your hands.
At first, as I slept, you
were the murderer
and I was breathless,
failing in arms that would end me,
my voice thrown in that absurd
combination of syllables
saved
for the truly holy.

II.

The wet season came
through milkweed
and arethusa of the lake.
As I sank,
one hundred bog orchids
threatened the air.
This sleep becomes
the watering stone
where we meet,
where I find you knee high
in yellow grass, pink callused hands
tracing the brackish
movement of crows through trees,
bare feet caked with algae,
your conductor's pose.

III.
Where were we
two thousand years ago
when the city I dream
swallowed a hot gasp of ash
that changed an evening,
perfect for pressing grapes,
into suffocation,
the archeology of a photograph
like memory:
a company of skeletons crouched
so close, they share
the same heap of ribs in death.

IV.
Dream this: our ruins have been re-figured.
Your war taken to bed
and sprung in a swamp of purple flowers
that lace your breath sweet and thick
as though Vesuvius had never raged
nor its force ever slung a woman
named Portia
through her clay roof, cast her down
shattered at the sea front.

V.
We pass through our place sometimes
in the day's orange end,
count the disasters
we find each other with,
the watering stones where we meet.
Tonight, I look for you in the ordinary.
I look in the boat house,

look for you gathering seaweed
on a rim of beach beyond that point
where birds search out
snails in green moss. I look long
before the mountain crumbles, burns.

Instruction

Three days and counting now
until their faces are before me
wanting what I can't give,
the moment learning becomes
real, saturates their clothes,
their hair. Kicks them hard
and says, yes. *You know
nothing.* I want to instruct them,
say: Unfold the impossible bundle
of messages before you,
take each one, carefully,
softly as though it may disperse
into a cloud of dust, the fleeting
stuff of moth wing,
of your own breath only this morning.
Unfold each with the care of a girl
finding for the first time
the pungent smell of hard work
on her own skin, wanting it
again, and again. Smooth and unfold
each until you have found in the center
the white circle of a page, blank
as the utterance of your own name.
Before you forget what you have,
put all you find into your mouth
and swallow. Swallow hard. Swallow
the whole thing, not a thing, and mean it.

Esu Speaks the Moon

You may say the world bears my sacrifice
in the wooded moment of a noon turned sour
because the sky pretends she is really
stark and cold,
although we know
in evening, she loves us
without knowing our names.
Even though you are a husband,
pretend you are Esu
and your hands are the only thing
between us,
your eyes, the long path toward
this bed
where you've watched me
search for breath and a moment
of being. I will not leave you
even if that means your haunting:
my voice
in the shower
when you touch the soap,
in the mirror when you drag the comb
over your soft scalp
wondering
what myth could heal you.
I have conjured up an ancient god.
I have found the secret of this room.
Each evening is a trick we fall for,
a momentary sigh of the universe
that spins us into a blind forgiveness.
Believe me. Believe the constellations when they
scatter their messages over your eyes.
Your hands and my hands have never been
so full of each other.

Odyssea Home

What are the patterns of a dark room
we see despite our failing eyes,
the mute messages sent without light?
The answer matters less than the weather
until they declare a state of emergency
in the face of sleet and storm.
Suppose you are broken,
everyone is trapped again,
nowhere to go.
Even a tirade of water and wind
could conjure up the anger of the sea
spitting ancient vessels from her belly
like a storybook troll
coughing the bones of children out
with laughter. I think now
Calypso was not a hero.
I think I can live without apples
and pears if I need to.
I could live without turnips.
I could survive without oranges
or Africa or Greece.
I am nothing there.
But I keep the dream of a woman
who signed rapidly in anger,
her face twisted past the ocean,
the blue eyes that swallowed her,
as though no sound was instead
a brother who loved
the idea of her pressed lips,
and an old lover, in death,

who followed her transparently
through the rooms of her house
as though his mute longing
could unshadow her silence.
Somewhere in my past,
they're throwing an old woman
out of her home because she's sick
and chanting the songs of her
neighborhood. She sees her husband
trimming lilacs, her sons
fighting near the stream
and rapidly mouths their names.
Bastards, bastards, every one.
Sometimes, words are simply
too accurate for anger and lust
unless rage is a thrust
of the arm, a turned mouth,
the brow folded in.
Suppose still, you are broken.
You could once cure everything
with salt or butter, sometimes
a bleeding, but pretend now
sound will fix us
to the graves of our youth,
the tide behind us, the hiss:
sister, lilac, sea.

The Carpenter's Dream

If a man abide not in me, he is cast forth from the vine and is withered.
                                            —John 15:5

I.

> I am there, with him. He yells to a mule.
They begin. A slow grind of wheels spins forward on round
> > stones
while gutter flow streams the west side berm. He is awake.
His heart thunders lungs into their fight
so that each limb folds into the fall.

> How has this happened?
He knows few things: a plank of wood remembers the hands
which plane the form whole, that find straight lines.
A hand can learn each knot in a grove of olives,
pull breath from the grain, or summon a cheek,
a chin smooth as a boy waking
his long dream of roots.

II.

> He remembers a day he never knew.
Winter storms move towards Sulmo into trees
that leave their roosts. A flock of women lose
the shelter of a cave where boulders rake a slope into cliff.
Above their heads, a birth of bats shaken out of their nests
forms an eclipse of wing.

> Are these the others, two men who kneel,
start a fire from flax and new timber? Behind them,
three goats hang from their hind hooves and bleed
blank stares into the dirt. The men laugh, as thieves do,

into flames which draw black furrows from their ribs.
Tonight, they are brothers and in sleep
confess crimes even they do not remember.

III.
He searches again, desperate for this man,
carves out arms, allows the eye open
beneath a brow span of one hand,
wounds the grain with a chisel
where the mouth should be.
The neighbors chant.

He makes doors for all the homes in Rome . . .

someone says, and he remembers, again, as if he knows
the pitched calls of women's grief for his own voice,
a sound of many waters in the day revealed.

Today a cat wails, a boy shouts his father's name,
devotion follows an expedition of women
bringing their white shrouds back from the well.
The carpenter dreams my dream. *The wood forgives me.*
He knows one less thing.

At 57, My Father Learns to Grow Things

I prepare to go to the islands,
buy hats, and bathing suits, flippers
that will push even my large body
carelessly through too blue water.
Two thousand miles away, my father sits on his porch,
watches his land, the whole acre
stretched like a small corridor through birch
and aspen sprung from Pennsylvania culm.
He has, just now, discovered the soil,
how it responds to water and spikes of plant food,
tells me by phone each Sunday the inventory of life:
three green tomatoes, radishes, cucumbers,
melons for the grandkids, zucchini everywhere
but the golden ones, not green. Six months before
I visit for Christmas and find myself, 16 and slim,
(a photograph in haste as I cringed at the camera)
there on his nightstand. I'm suddenly struck
by my own absence in his house, even within
my presence—I am gone. Now, while looking
one more time at the glossy magazine of my island,
the stucco balcony where I'll split papaya,
I am jealous of the tomatoes in my father's yard,
the strawberries that ignore their small pots and root anyway
as he protects them with mesh and clanking cans,
turquoise fertilizer that looks like the sea I run to.
I can only ask him to send me brussels sprouts,
carefully packed so the long journey will not cause rot.
I can only savor them when they arrive
like a success between us that closes and opens
the long distance home.

The Migrant

>   . . .*Women become*
> *The cities, children become the fields*
> *And men in waves become the sea.*

>   —Wallace Stevens

I.

First time I saw another
brown face: Aunt Janie's farm.
She rents it and the workers come
up from the South, slow moving
sun in the limbs, to pick the landlord's
fields, pick the landlord's tomatoes
while all their children
stare, wondering why,
why this girl like them
dirty at the knees and ashy—
nappy headed sits in the yard
and they
lay their bellies in a row
snaked outside the fence,
a row of soybean, row of corn
watching me swing.
She sits on the swing.
Where you come from, girl
like us. Where you goin' now?

Her migrant children rush
   the porch steps
where tomato skins are kicked and split
by feet returning to where the life
   has kept her migrant.

Across the way
in the field, I see
this woman, head wrapped
in bluish grey.
I'm sweating
just like her and she bends,
so I bend.
She reaches into the tomato patch,
stands and wipes
the back of her hand against
her forehead,
the hand that holds the tomato,
too ripe.
I stand
and wipe my hand against
my face, pretend
to be tired from picking
so many
tomatoes and I swear,
just then she turns. The road
turns between us, turns narrow
and she looks over,
looks right at me, eye on eye.

Children rush the porch, their steps
galloping madly, maddening,
*   a herd adept to the earth as a hand to the hilt of a hit.*
Her children rush to the porch, just five wooden steps,
seizing baskets of tomatoes to kick and split.

II.
I hide in the barn all day
sneezing from the chickens.
Outside, the afternoon

has hated me,
baked me brown
and lazy into this corner
where the darkness
wraps her arms around me,
clammy sister's arms,
empty but open.
From the porch my name
carves a trajectory through the yard,
Ruthellen, Ruthellll-ennnn
as though my mother
in a moment away from the warm
tongue of coffee and peach pie
just realizes her longing.

Slowly the woman moves her braids
away from her sweating maplewood face
while the landlord's cows bend to graze.

I pretend I am the migrant's child
and the white lady on the porch
calls some other girl, calls
into the barn, hoping
for some other girl.

The woman moves, her braids
a twisted pepper-salt maze
of a black woman's nappy, too-shamed lace.
As she moves, her braids
fall away from her maplewood face.

III.
I go to the house
to pose for a family picture.

My cousin,
years before he would hold me down
angry that he'd become a man,
is now happy with his trucks
and cake, and birthday cards,
wraps his long arm around my neck
and pokes my ribs at the flash
so that later
I am the scowl in a wash of smiles,
the dark dot in the photo
with hands touching,
hands all around her.

Her music is a portal, a dance,
two black hands beat the air,
the bold body shadow changes stance.

My mother kisses my hives and asks
if I've been playing
with the chickens and I turn away
knowing she knows so much more
than I've said. Through the window
the long procession of hired hands,
all women saddled with the faces of dark men
who became the faces of their own children
calling them as they move through the field,
move as if they wade water,
high waves
that cripple them into this movement,
legs lifted
knee high with each step.
The quarters open up to them,
white boxes with chimney stacks.

Her music is a portal of dance,
sweating skin, her feet tracing chance,
the body wheeled through air with the care
her music gives. A portal of dance,
two black hands beat air.

I have scratched
my skin into bleeding spots
and my mother dabs me pink,
calomined and sleeping,
as though pink can heal me.
She puts me to bed in my cousin's room
without my knowing how his hate
will someday take me in sleep,
a dry rhine of forgetting.
My girl she says and folds me in,
gives me back to darkness.

About the Author

Ruth Ellen Kocher was born in Wilkes-Barre, Pennsylvania in 1965. Shortly before receiving a Bachelor or Arts degree from Pennsylvania State University in 1990, she was a fellow at the Bucknell Seminar for Younger Poets. In 1994 she earned a Master of Fine Arts degree in poetry at Arizona State University where she will receive a Doctor of Philosophy degree in literature in the spring of 1999.

Her poetry has been published in such literary journals as *African American Review, Antioch Review, Gettysburg Review, Missouri Review*, which awarded her the Tom McAfee Discovery Feature, *Ploughshares,* and *Prairie Schooner.*

After numerous years in the American Southwest, she will relocate to Missouri in the fall of 1999 to serve as assistant professor of English at Missouri Western State College.

Desdemona's Fire is Ms. Kocher's first collection of poems.